CW01313733

© 2020 Sally Bignall Parenting Books. All rights reserved.

Hi, I'm Sally and I'm mum to two children. Raising them is such a mix of joy and exhaustion!

Perhaps you're just starting out; maybe you're an old hand by now but I hope you'll enjoy these observations and find them light relief!

For more family fun follow my Facebook & Instagram Pages 'Another UK mum'.

All the best with your parenting journey!

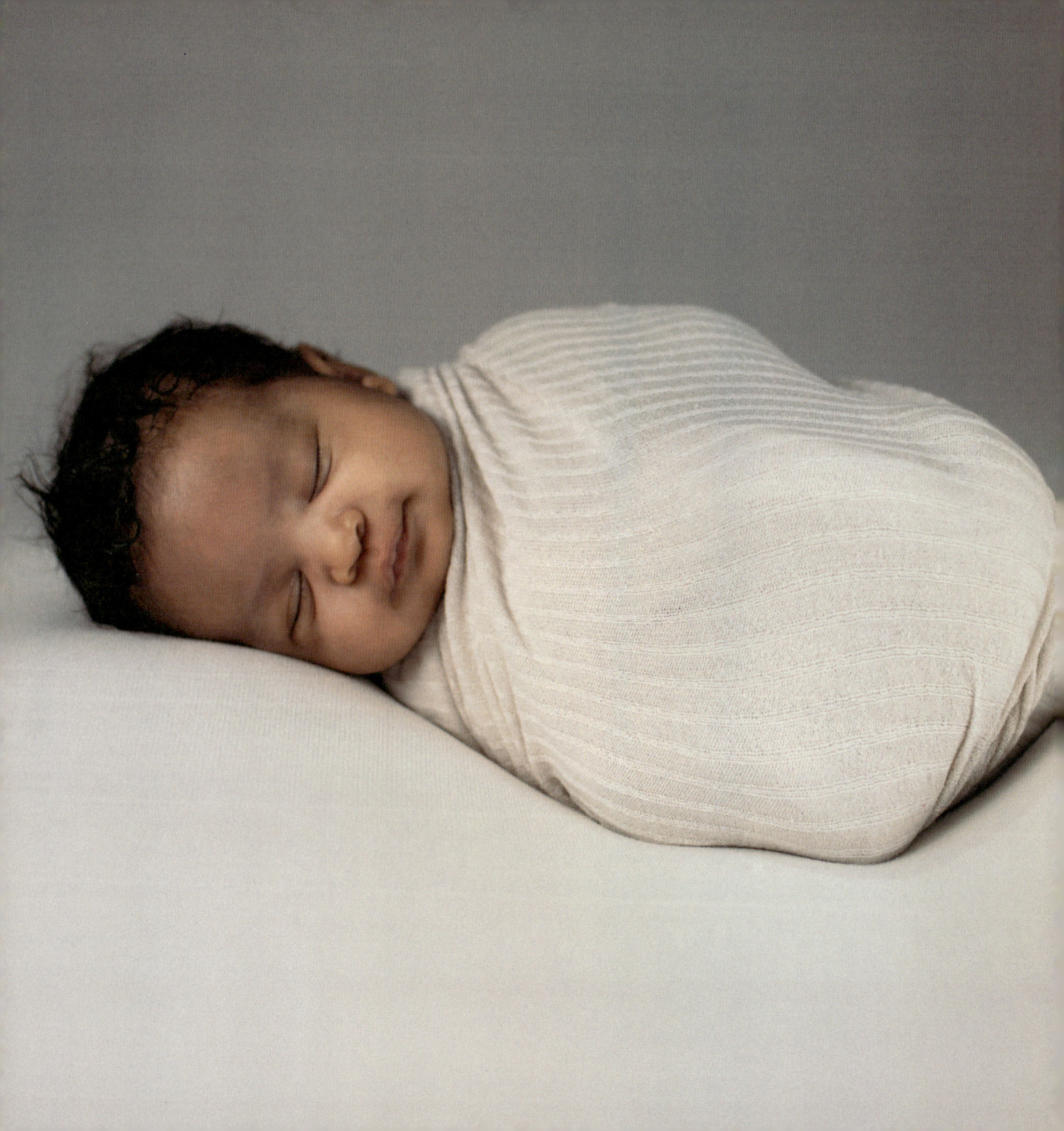

AH!

"What happened to my life?" Out with long lunches and savvy shopping and in with mother and toddler groups and serious saving.

AH!

Did you ever see such an adorable, gorgeous, amazing baby? Yes everyone thinks their baby is the cutest but yours really is.

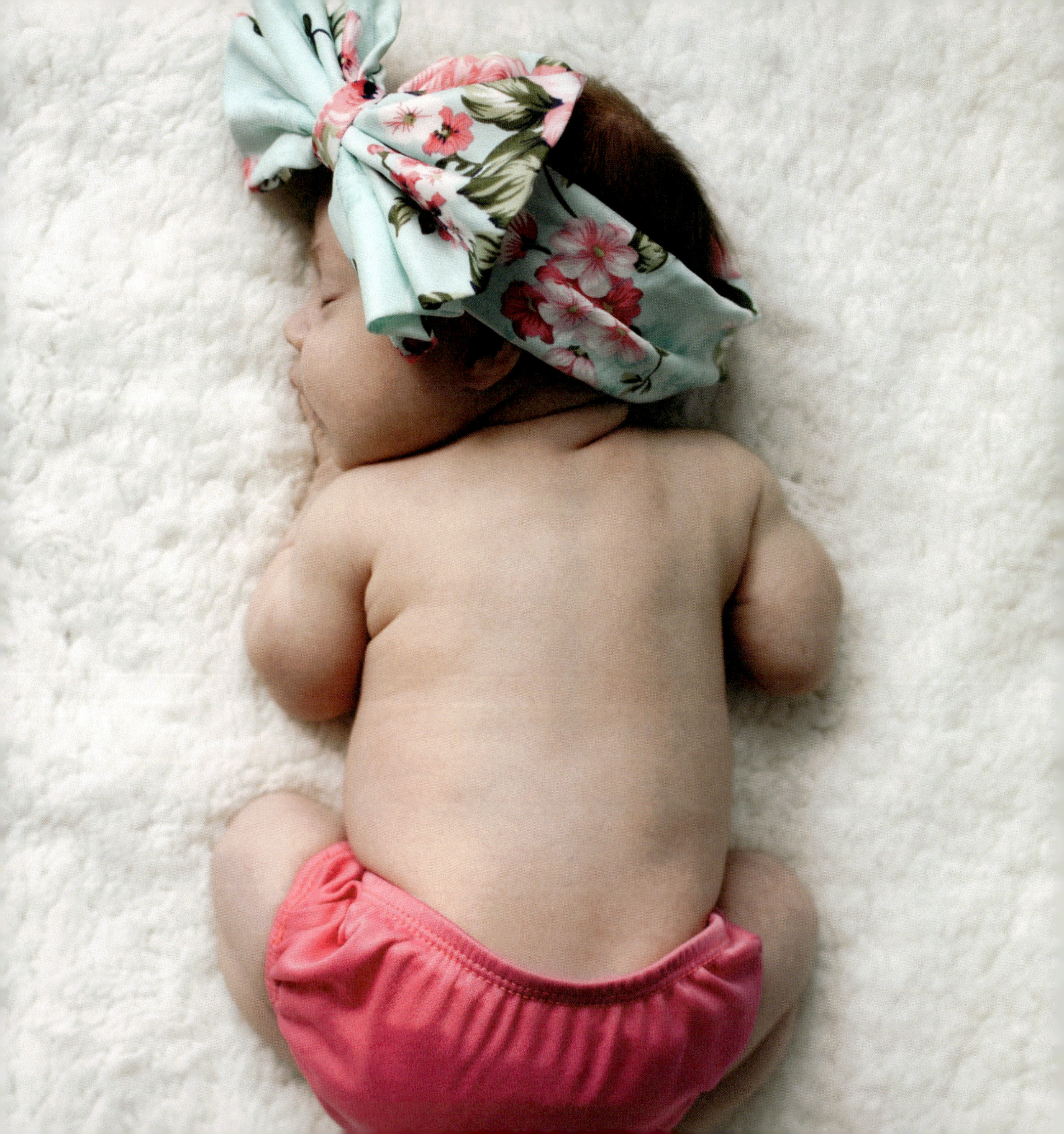

BOTTOM

No baby manual can prepare you for the variety of foulness that is expelled without shame or regard for present company.

BOTTOM

Peachy, cute and softer than your Favourite snuggle blanket.

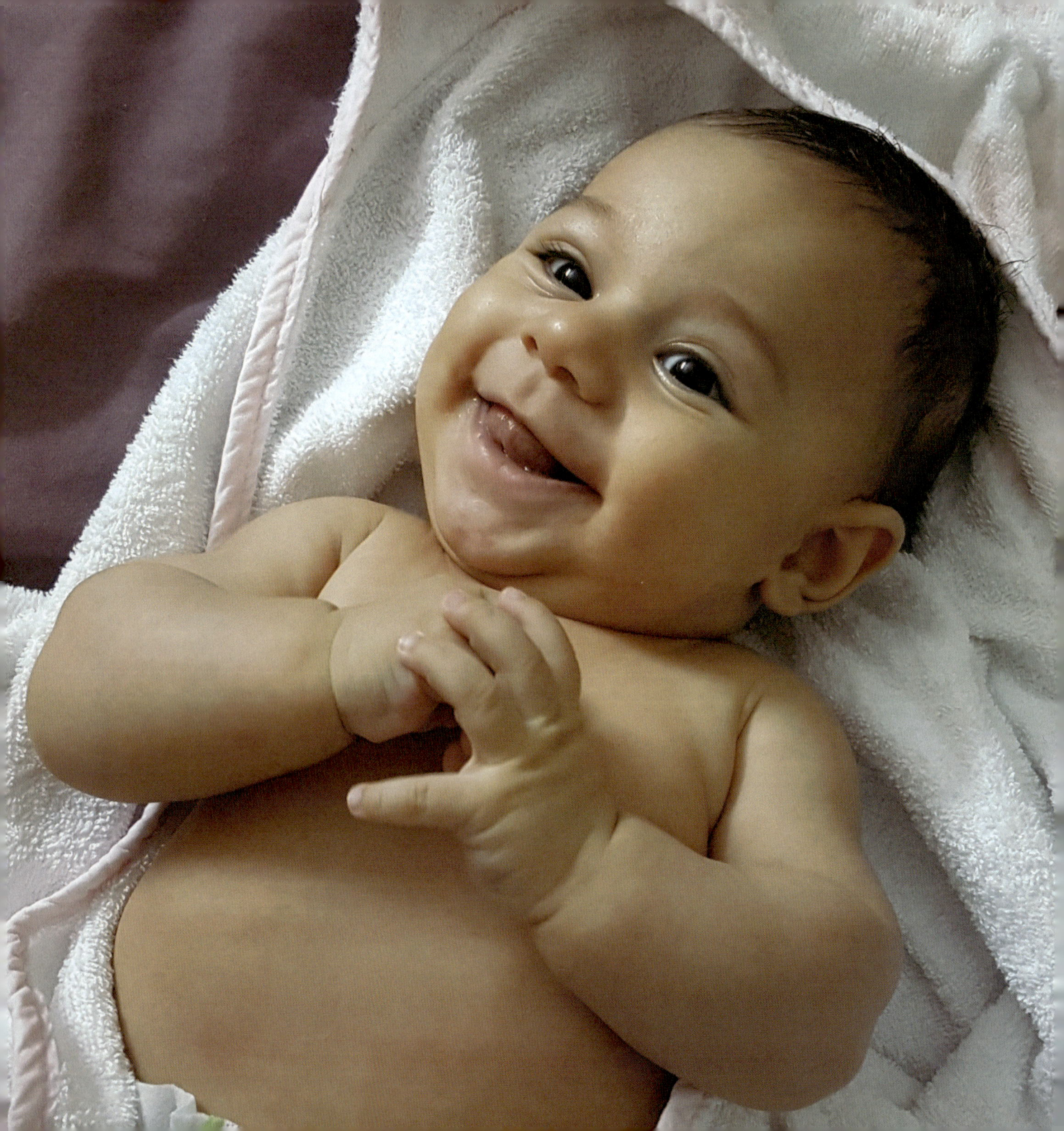

CUDDLES

Demanded constantly. Multi tasking at a whole new level as you go to the loo, get dressed and eat dinner one handed with baby clamped to your side.

CUDDLES

Got to be one of the best perks of the job. A cosy bundle of warmth nuzzled sleepily into your neck; you never want the moment to end.

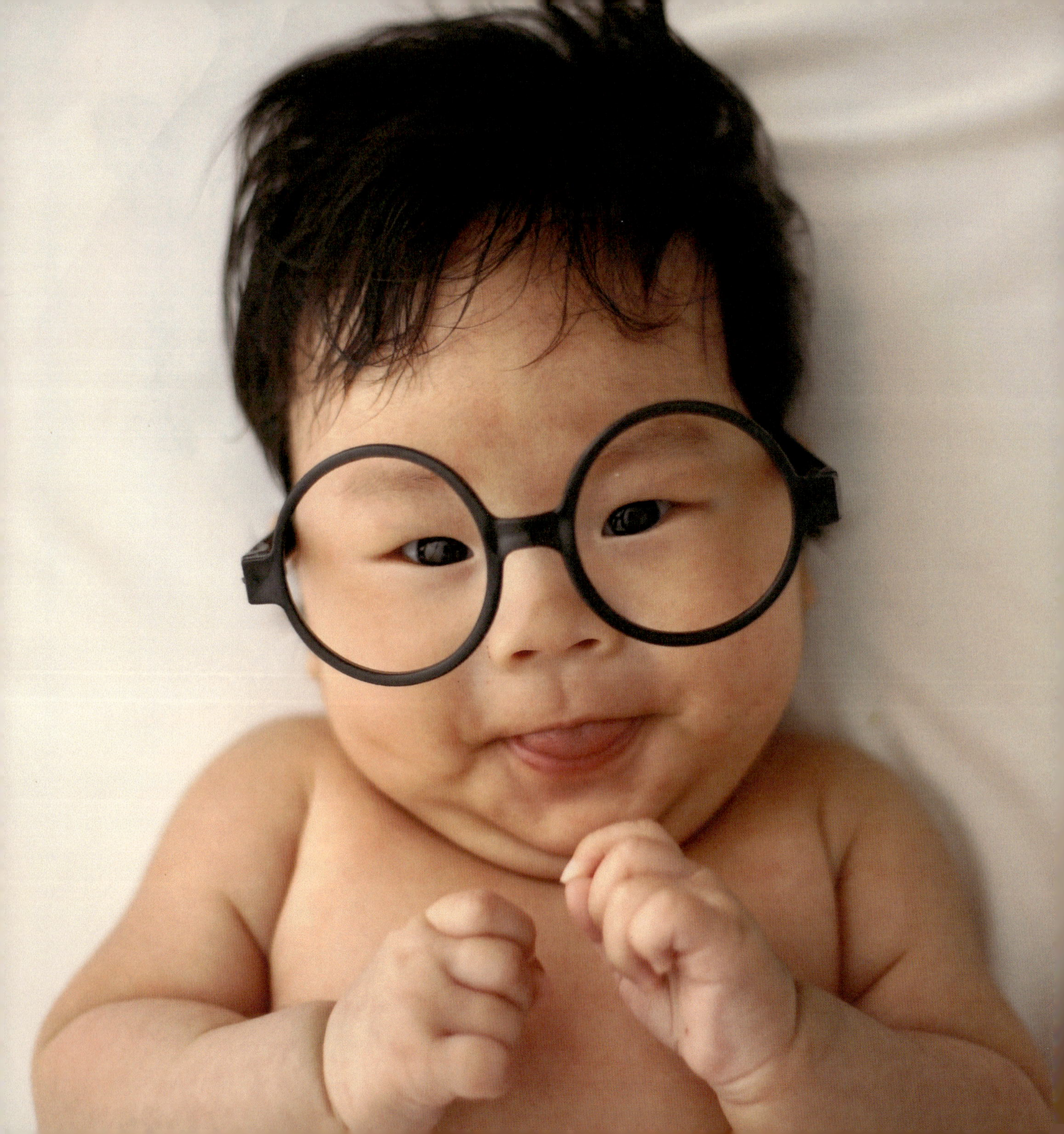

DOTING

Where have all your friends gone? Don't they want to spend every moment with you admiring every tiny fingernail and noting every milestone?

DOTING

Your finest hour. Your greatest achievement. Can you believe you created something so amazing!

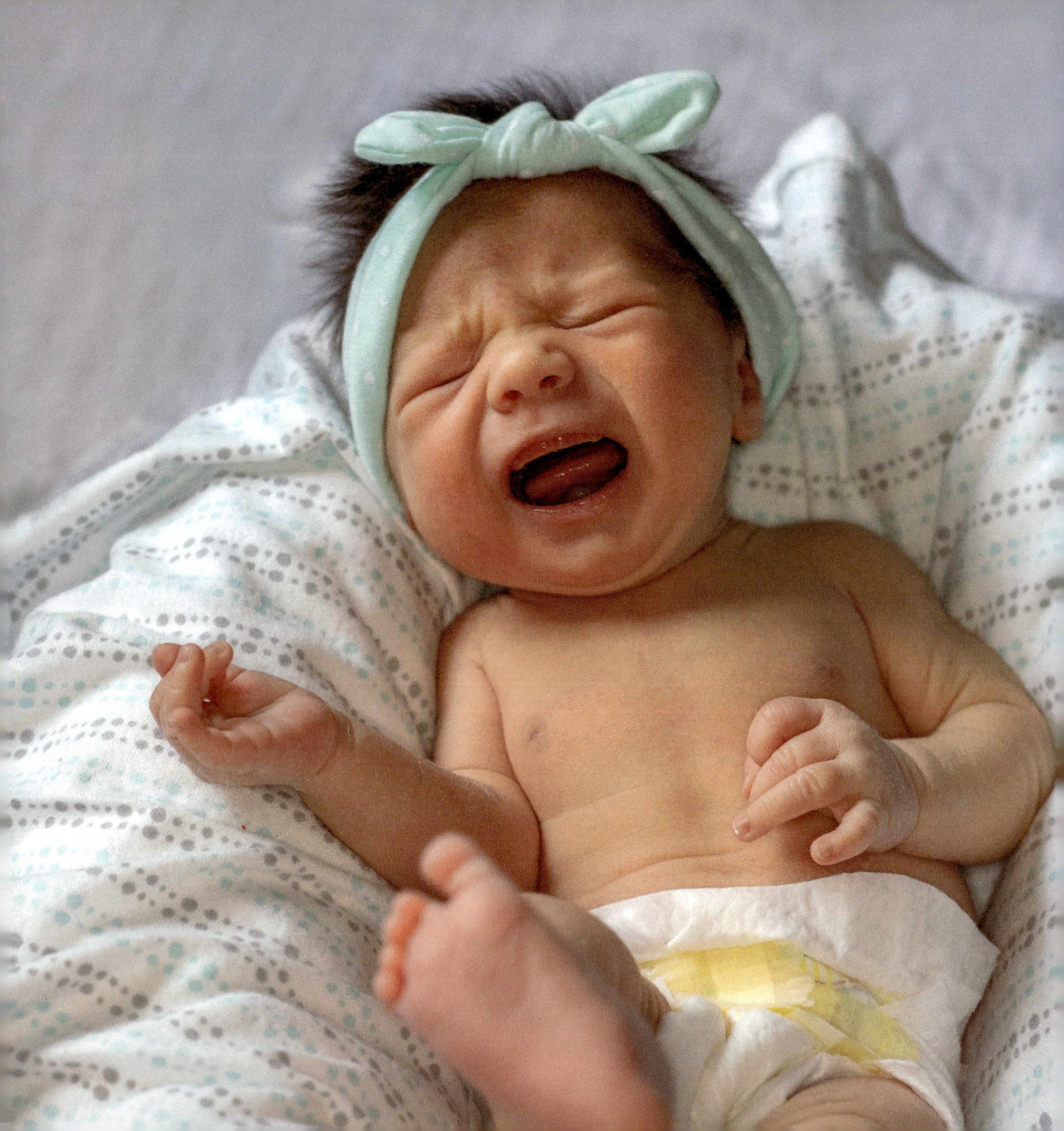

ENOUGH ALREADY!

24/7 on demand and not a hint of gratitude.

ENOUGH

Can't get enough of the smiles, the giggles,

the glorious extension of yourself.

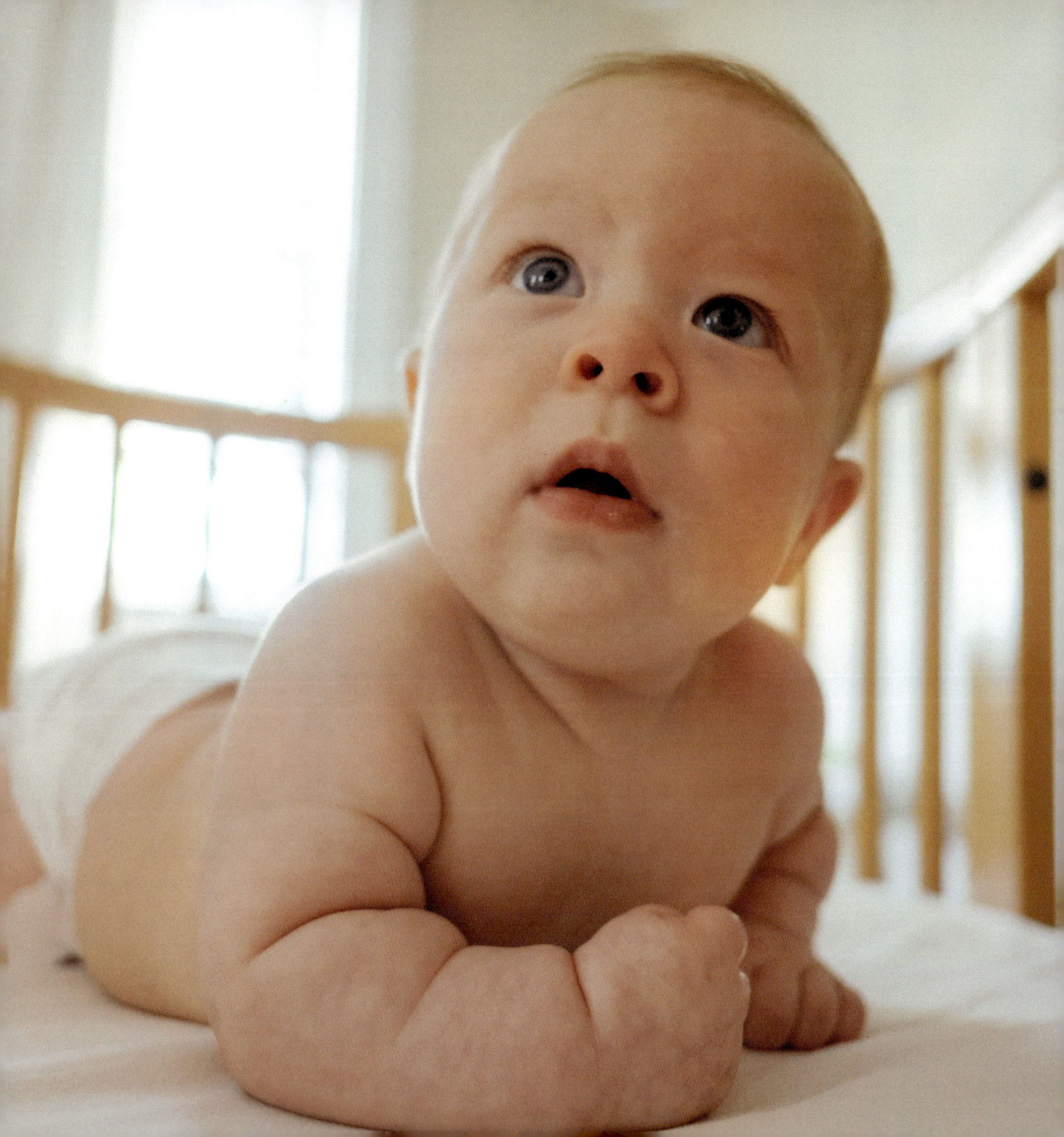

FOOD

From milk to "more!".

You've become an open all hours

food production factory.

FOOD

Whole new flavours to discover.

Chop, mash, boil and puree with organic produce

you never gave fridge space to before.

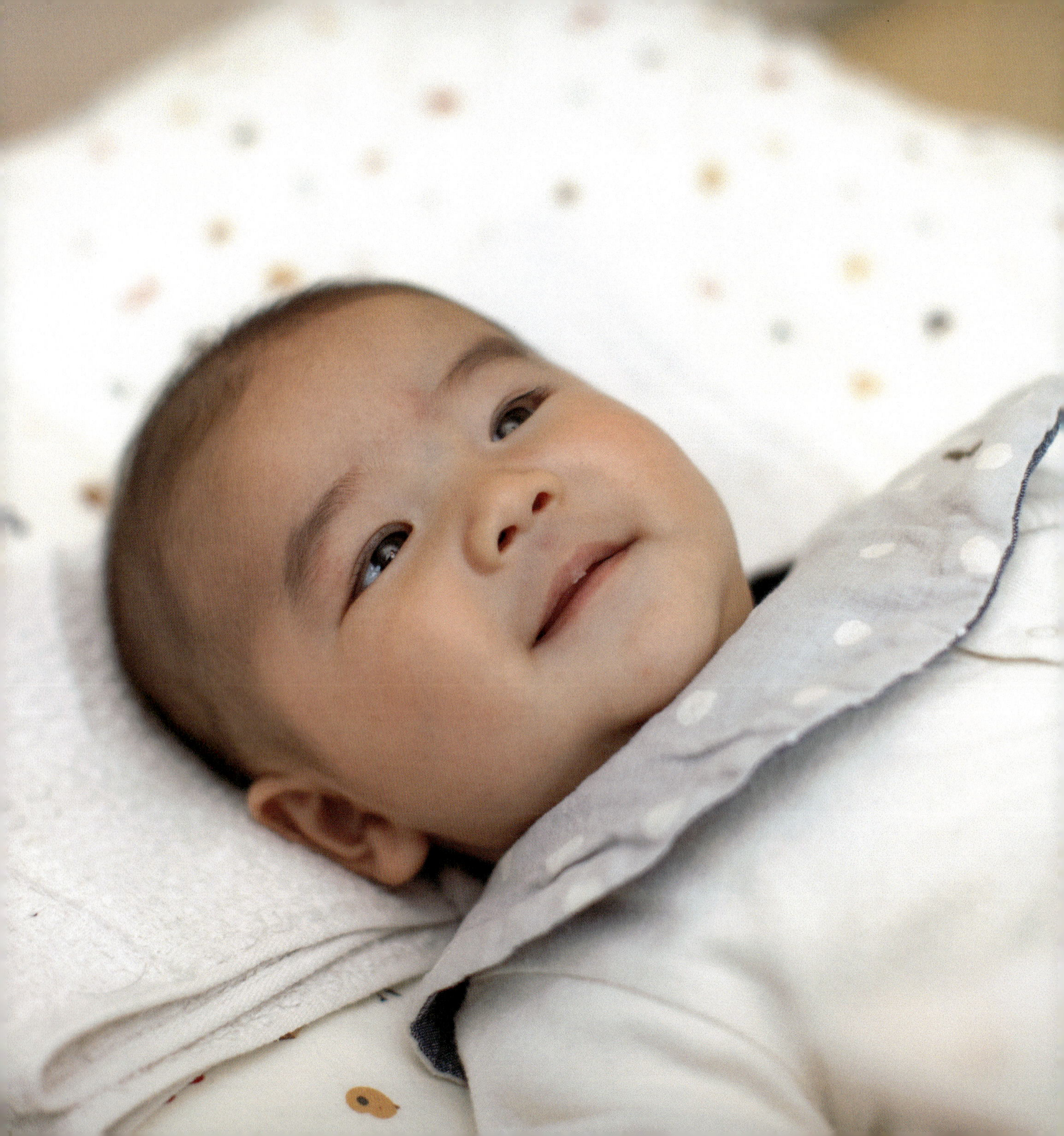

GRANDPARENTS

The only people who believe it is their natural right to undermine, overrule and generally disregard your carefully constructed ideology.

GRANDPARENTS

What would you do without them? Who else will insist you take time out while they share the joys and pains with as much relish?

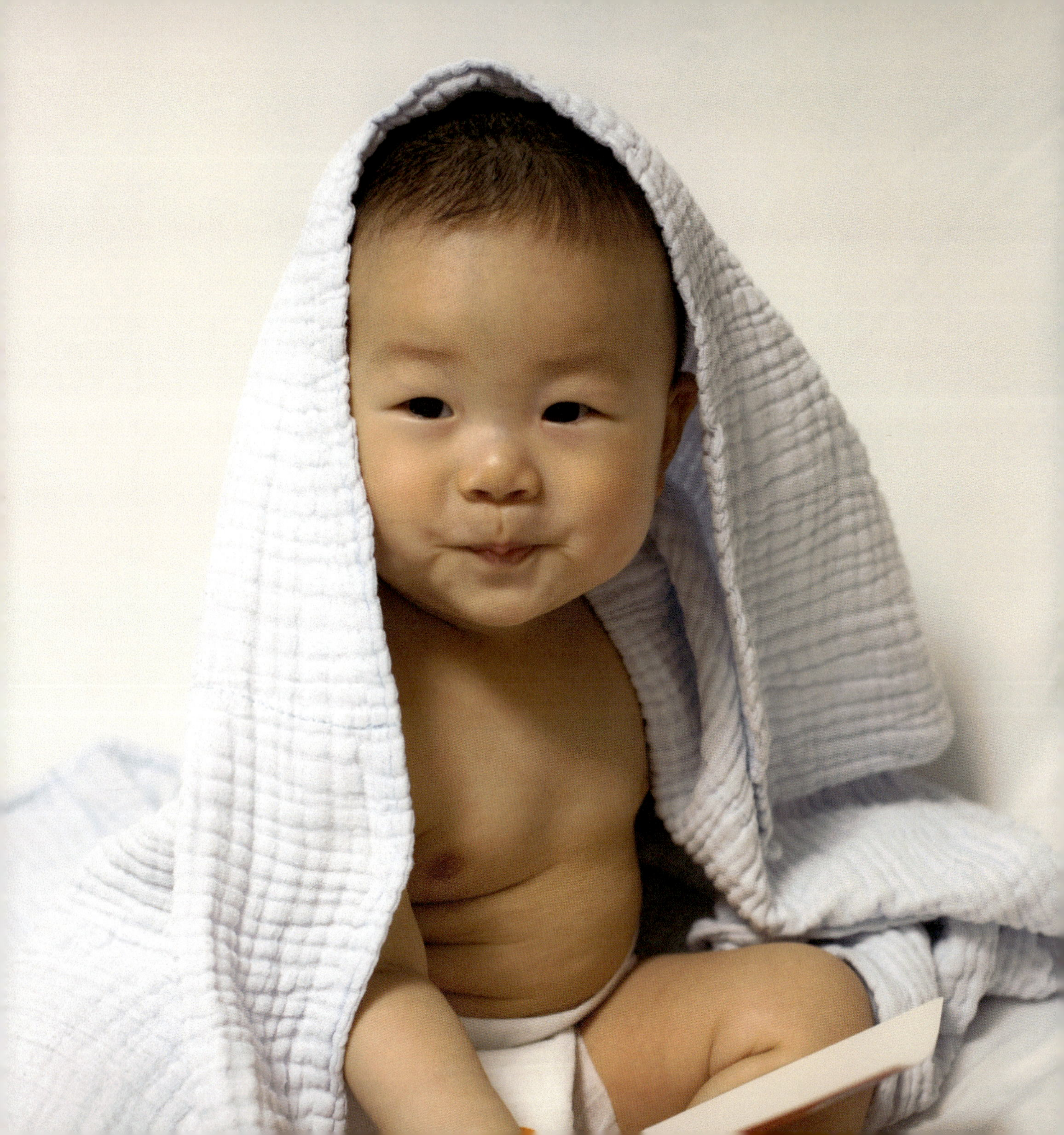

HOLIDAYS

Are now more work than being at home.
All that planning, packing and paraphernalia followed by early nights stuck in your room with only the mini bar to excite you.

HOLIDAYS

Whole worlds open up that have previously been off radar. Disneyland, 'kids go free' and anywhere with a soft play.

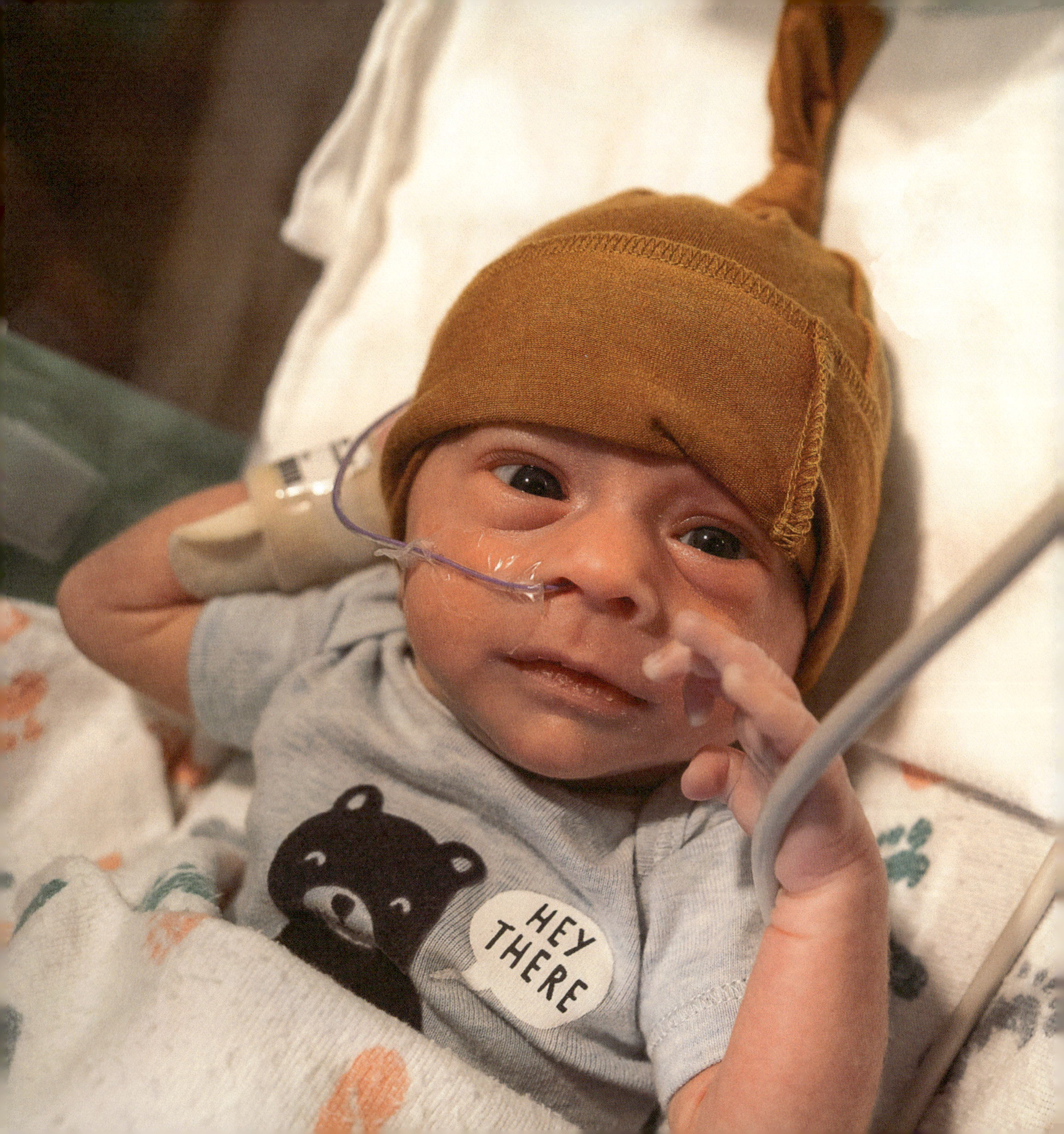
HEY
THERE

INDIVIDUAL

Refusing to conform to your plans, they set the pace and you have to bend or you'll break.

INDIVIDUAL

One of a kind with their own character, moods and expressions. You're constantly surprised and fascinated with who they are.

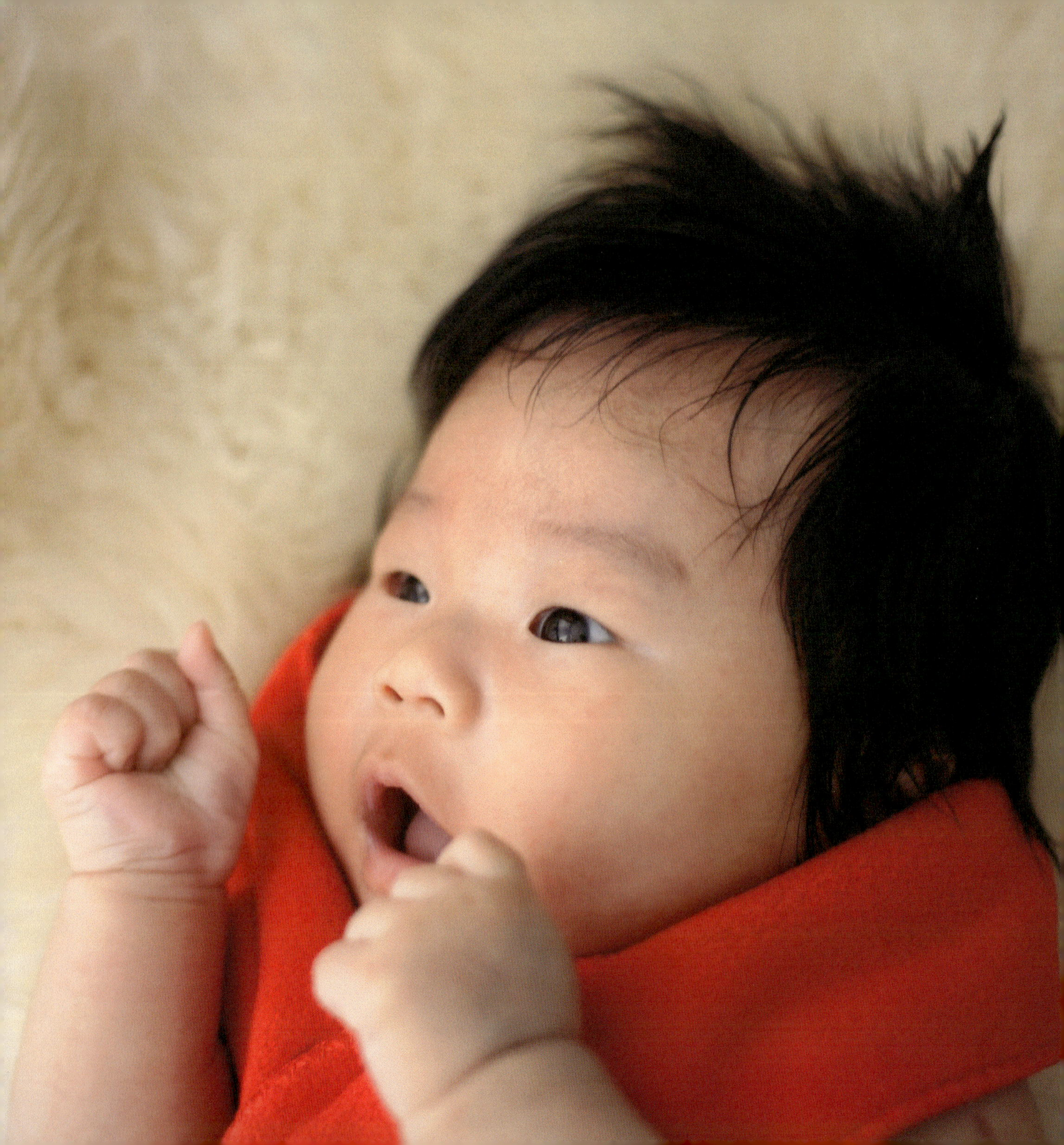

JABBER

Incessant babble. Peace and quiet are gone for good as a constant stream of noise accompanies your child.

JABBER

Every utterance is recorded and reported with huge pride. What joy when your baby begins to express themselves with actual words.

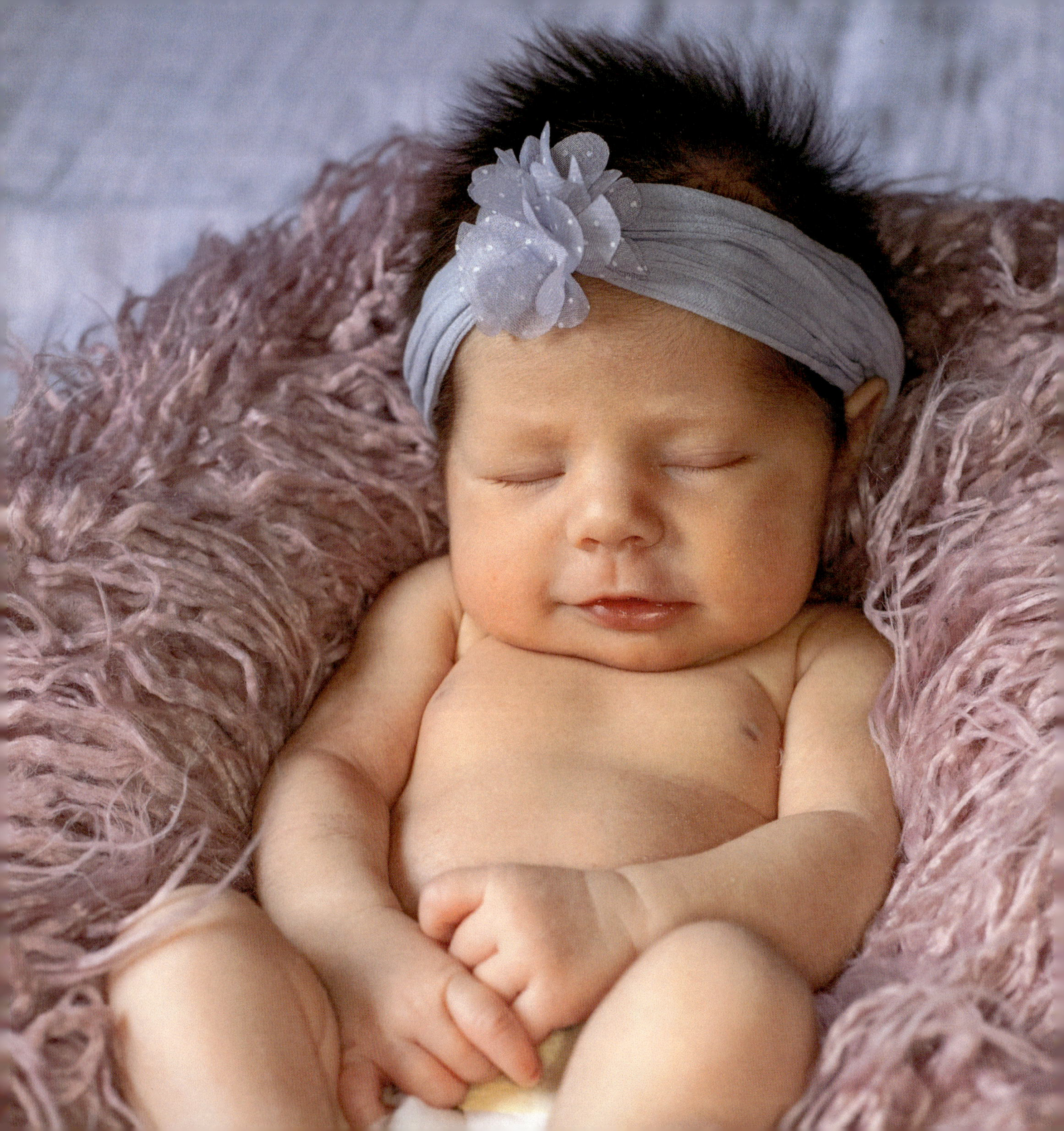

KILLER HEELS

You no longer get to wear killer heels.

Yes, you still buy them but you're too exhausted to ever get out there and show them off.

KILLER HEELS

You no longer have to wear killer heels.

Funky, comfy trainers are the footwear of choice from now on.

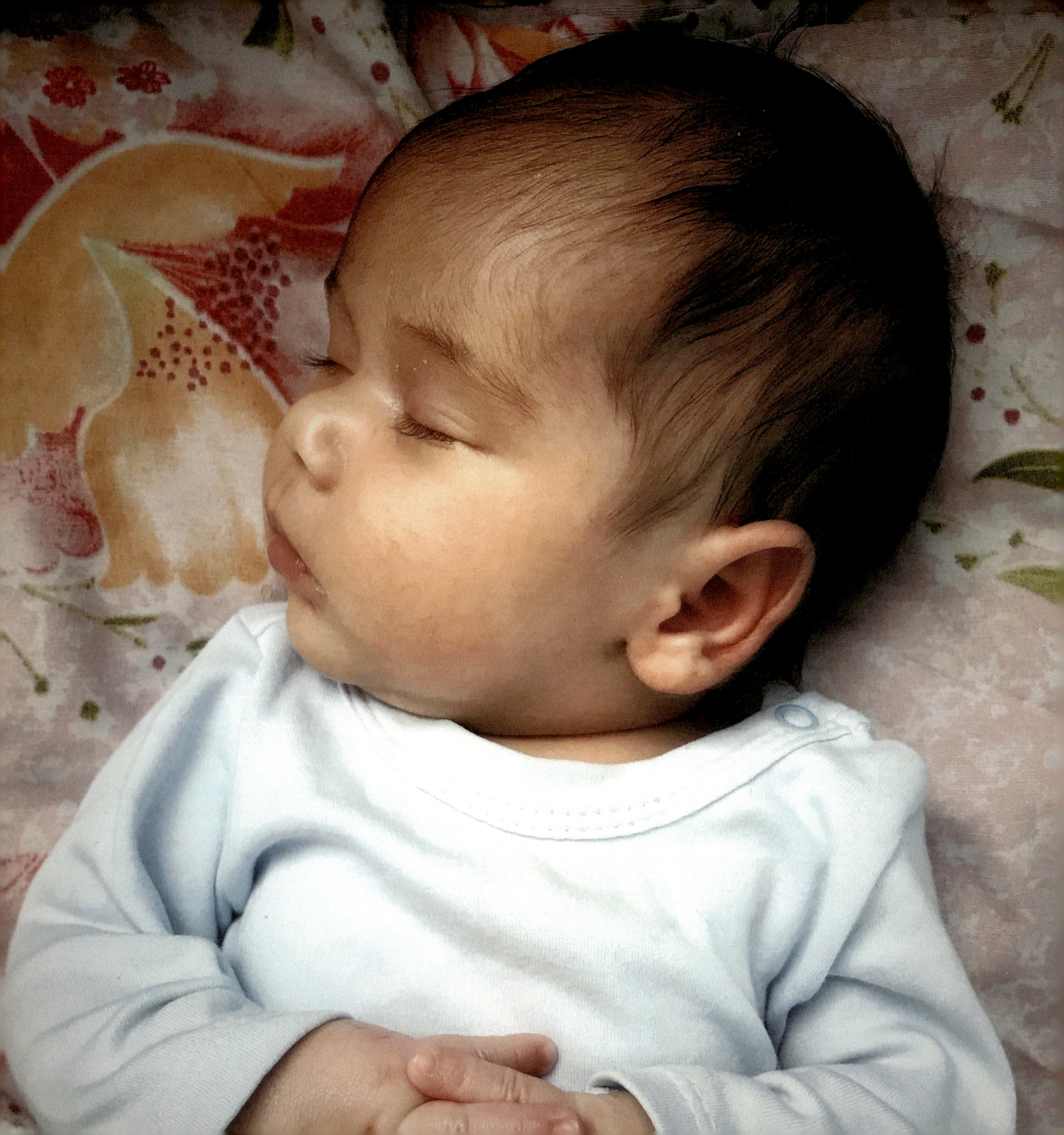

LOVE

It grabs you by the scruff of the neck and will never let go. You feel their pain almost as acutely as they do and are often powerless to take it away.

LOVE

Such unconditional love reserved exclusively for your baby...until child number two where you'll be astounded by your ability to multiply it.

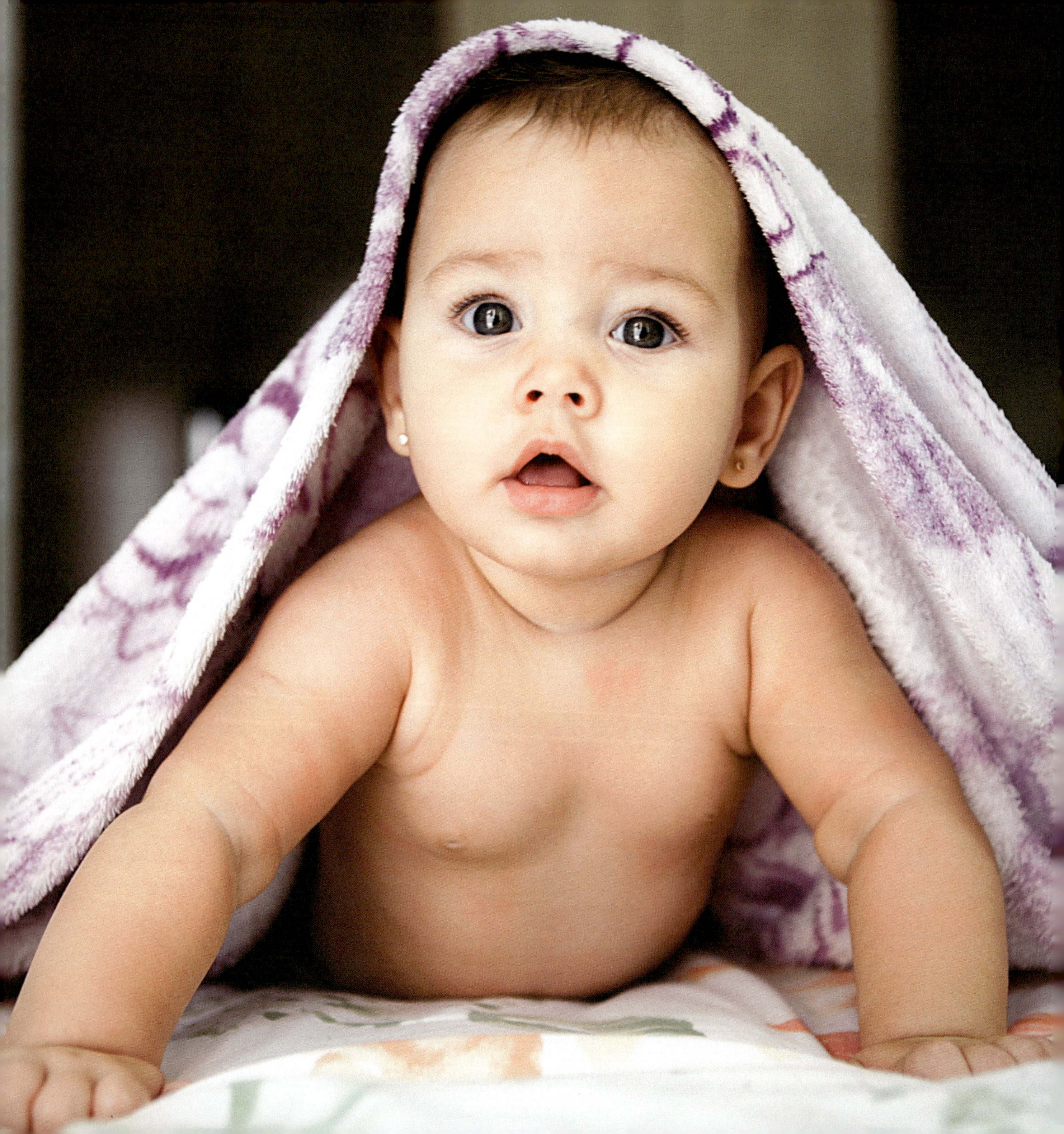

MOTHER & TODDLER GROUPS

Inane baby chat and petty competition can nearly drive you back to work just to find stimulation for your weary brain.

MOTHER & TODDLER GROUPS

A lifesaver for finding understanding friends to share your new, unfamiliar world.

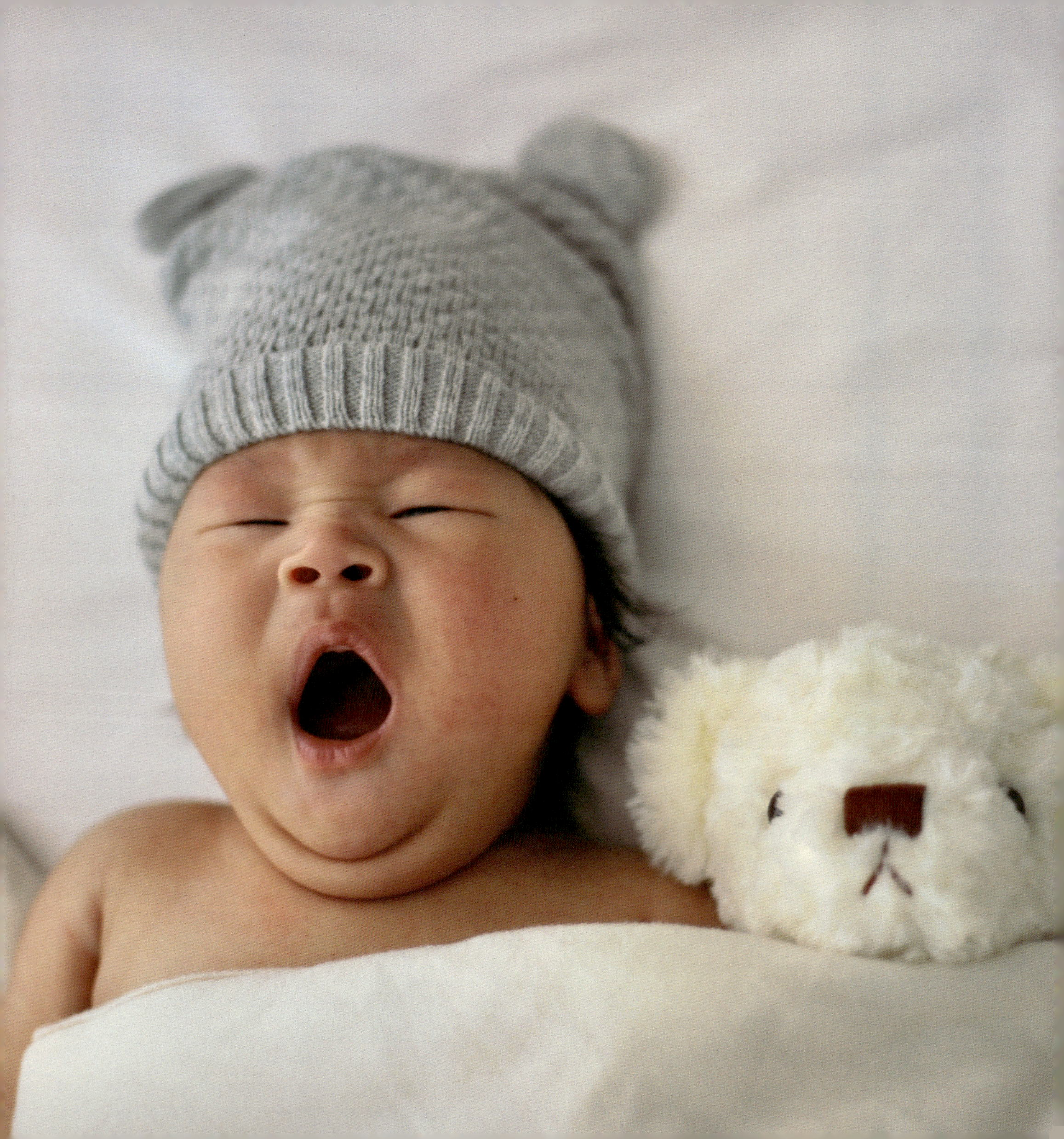

NIGHTS

Used to be for sex and sleeping.

Now they're for naps and feeding.

NIGHTS

Cosy nights in with your baby who's the perfect excuse to get out of a boring dinner party.

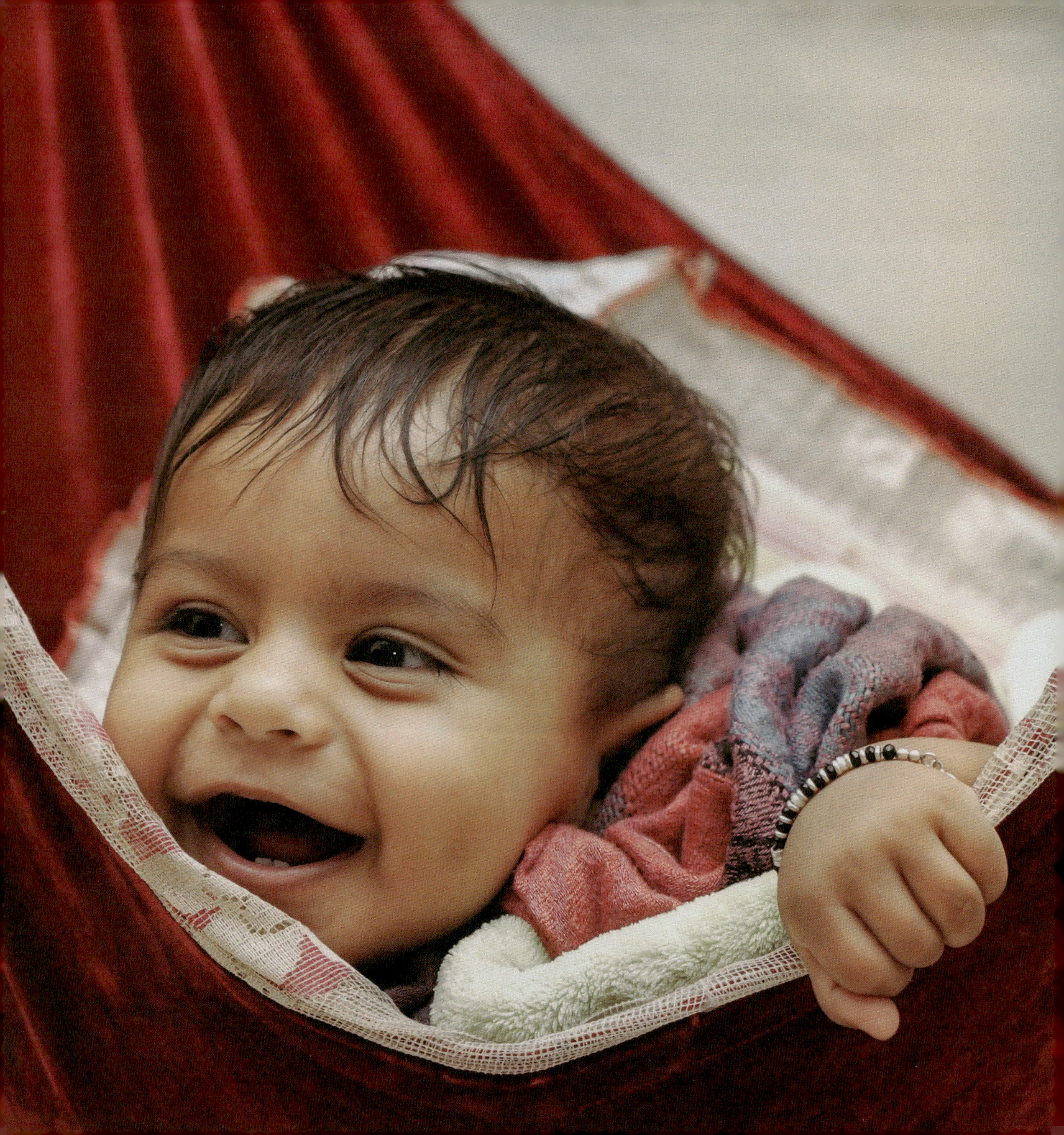

ORGANISE

The best laid plans are always at the mercy of your baby. Anything can happen and a change of plan is as common as a tantrum to a toddler.

ORGANISE

At last, your life is your own. No boss telling you what to do. Organise your life any way you want and take the time to think about the next chapter.

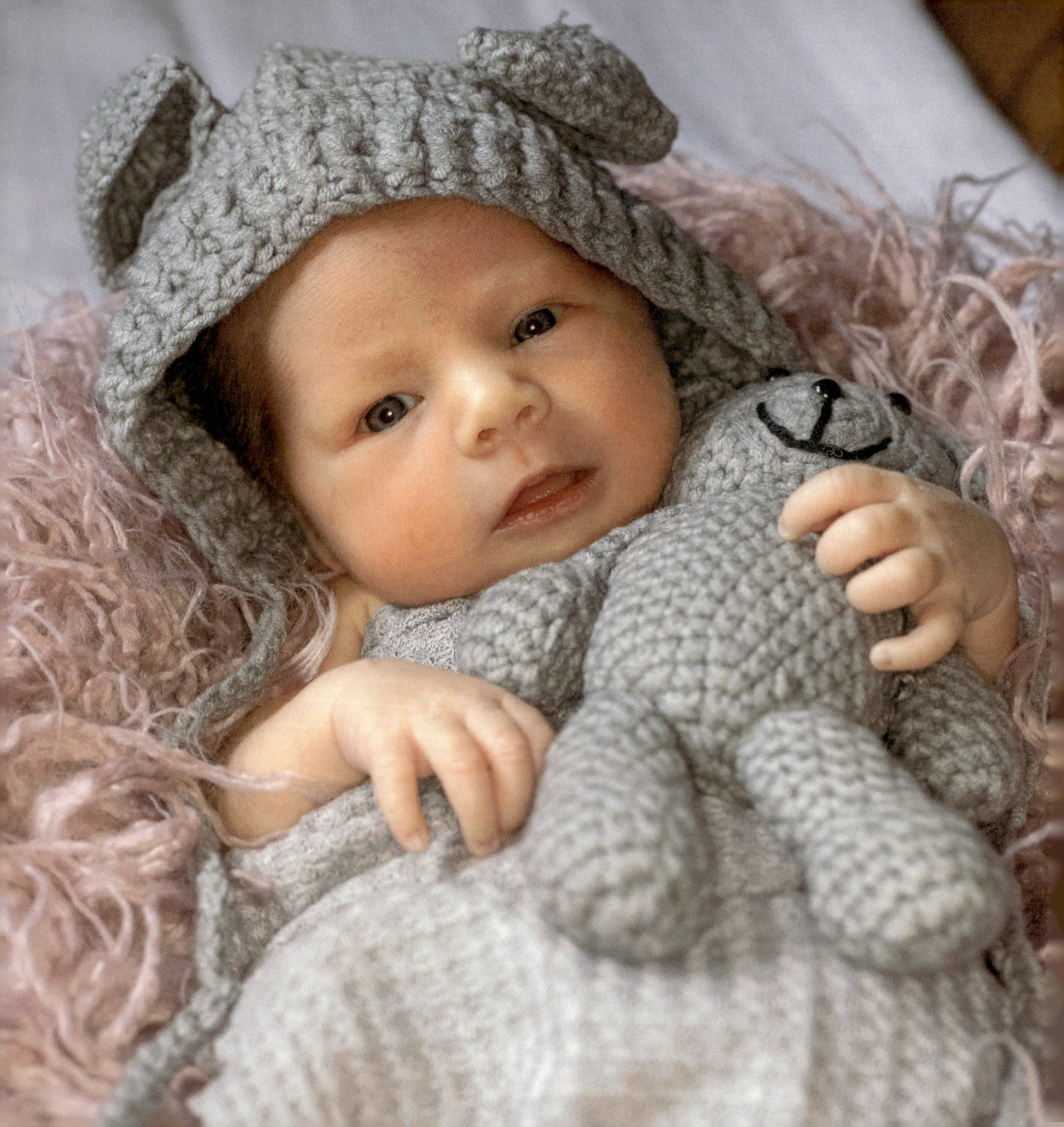

PARAPHERNALIA

Where did all the space go?

Every surface and floor is full of

baby baggage!

PARAPHERNALIA

So many new gadgets to buy,

so little guilt!

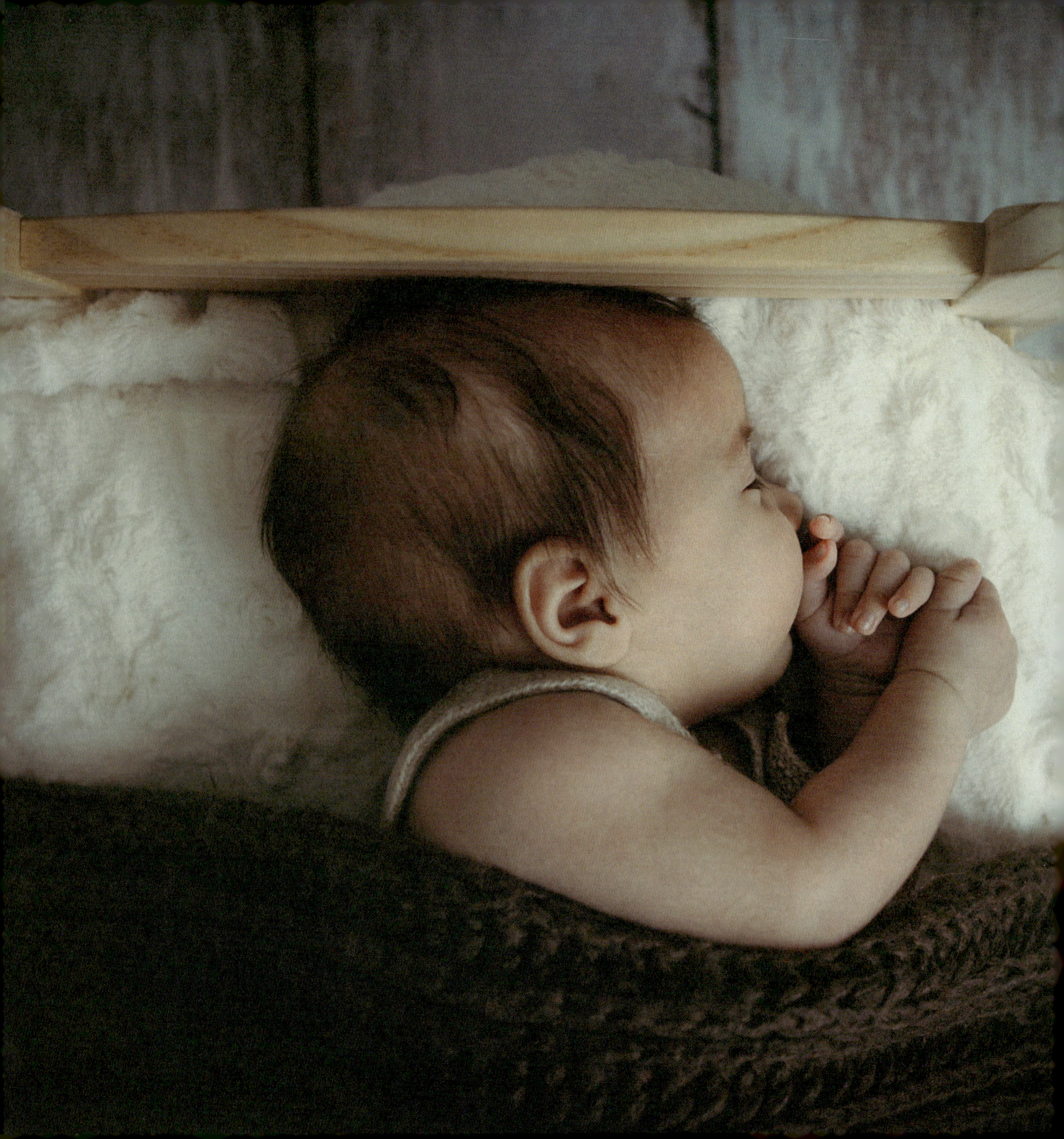

QUIET

Frantic moments skulking close to check for signs of breathing. You need to know all is well but can't risk waking your sleeping cherub and losing precious time out.

QUIET

Longed for and to be indulged with your favourite treats and time out.

The housework can wait.

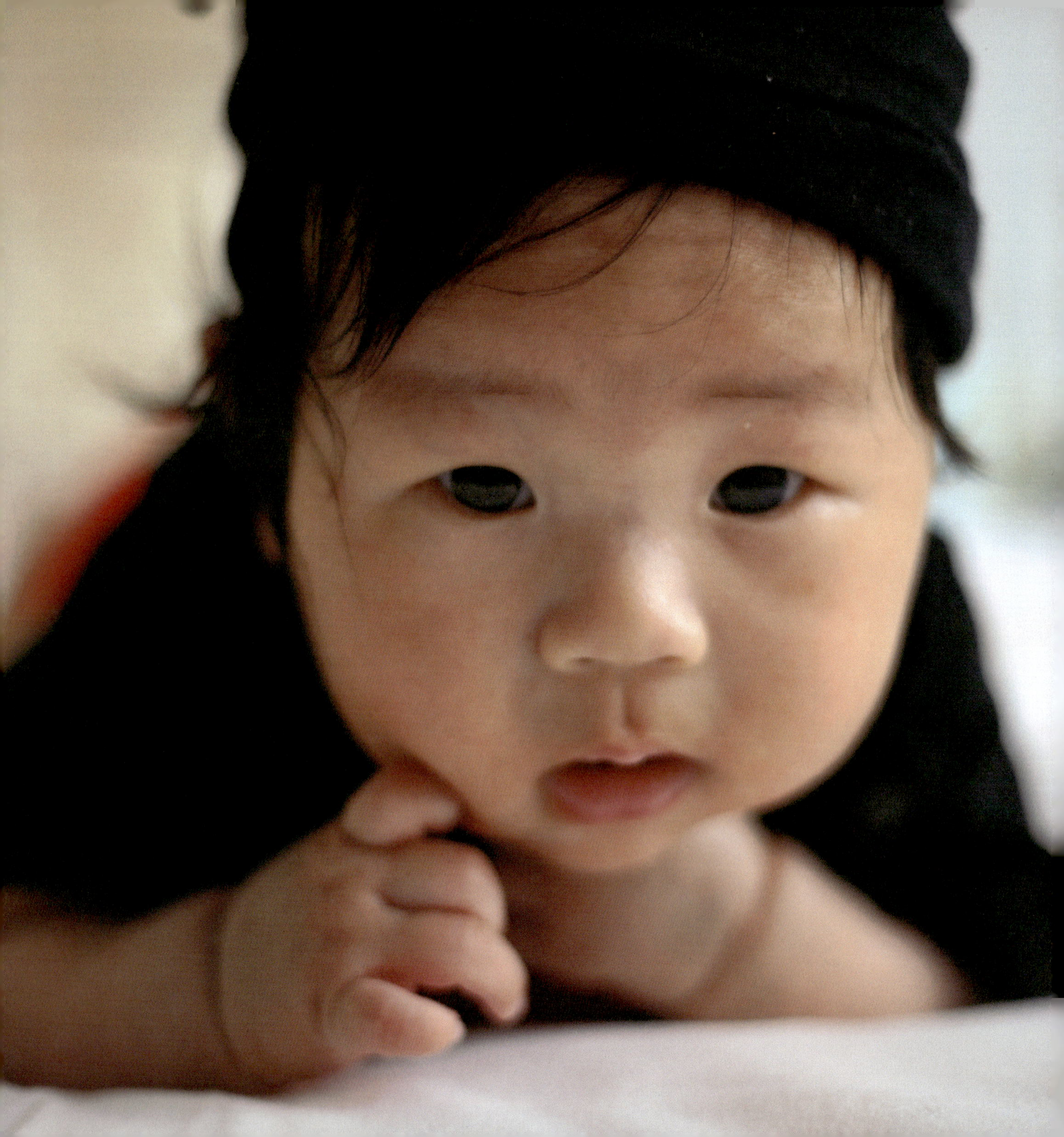

RELATIONSHIPS

Changing priorities can be threatening to partners and friends and sometimes these relationships need special care.

RELATIONSHIPS

A baby can deepen your relationship with your partner and enhance extended family bonds. Potential new friendships are everywhere.

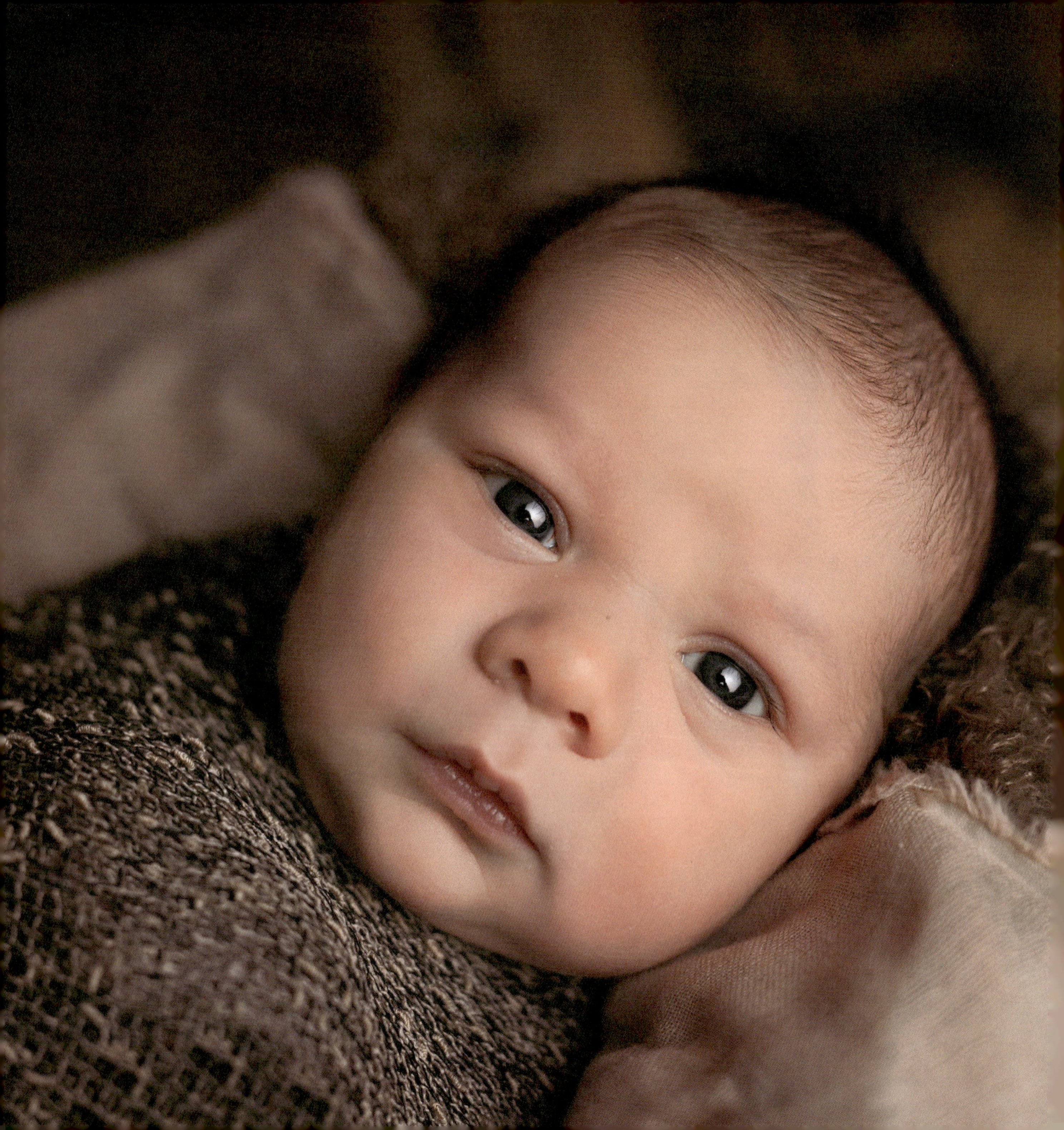

SMELLS

From nasty nappies to vile vomit.

What's that smell on your t-shirt?

Oh just some stale milky baby dribble.

SMELLS

Is there any better perfume in all the world

than the scent of your newborn baby?

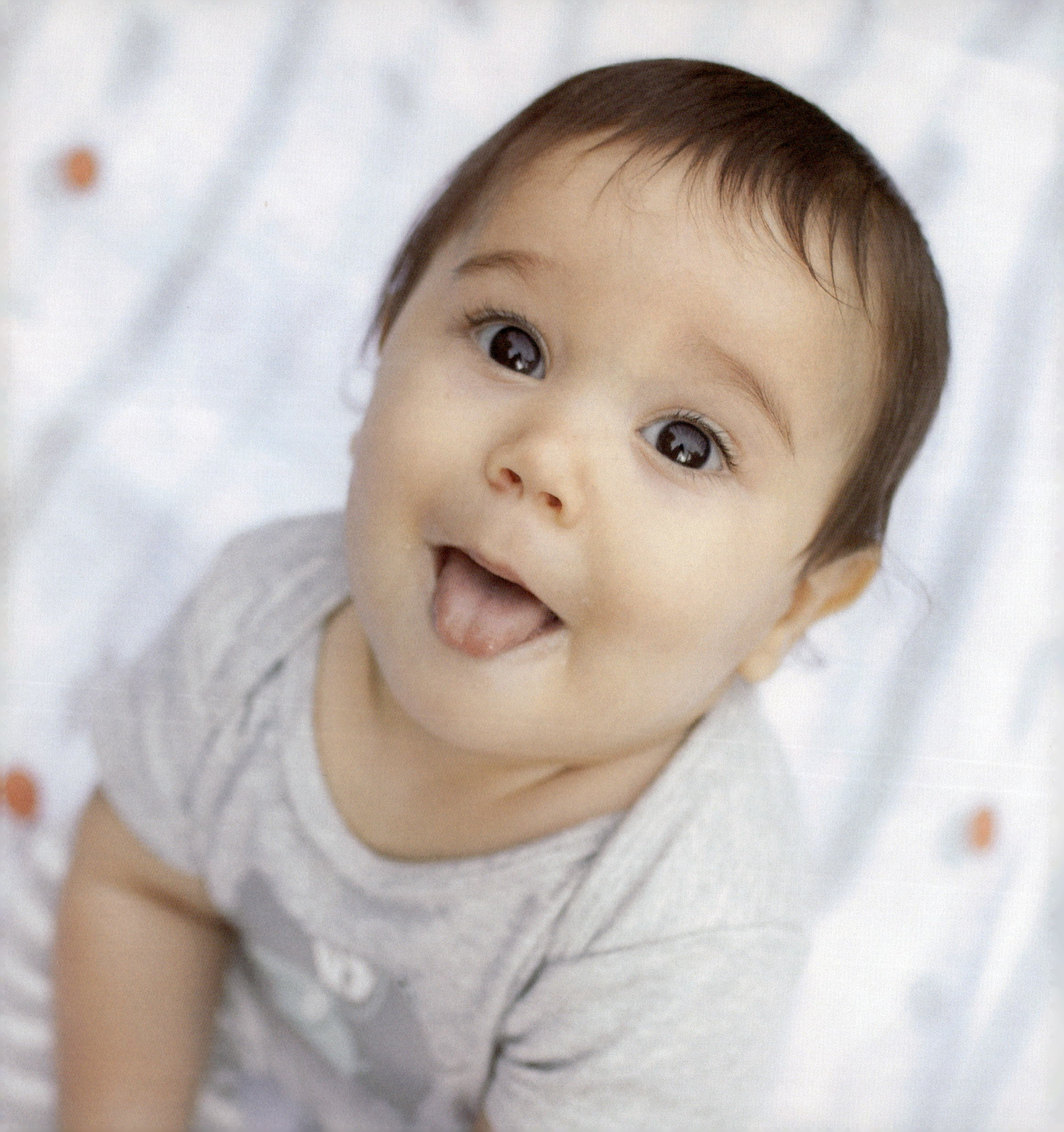

TEA

Unfinished brews litter the house.

Your baby has a sixth sense to cry

just as you add the milk.

TEA

There's nothing a nice cup of tea can't fix.

Relish that soothing brew when

baby is finally asleep and all is quiet.

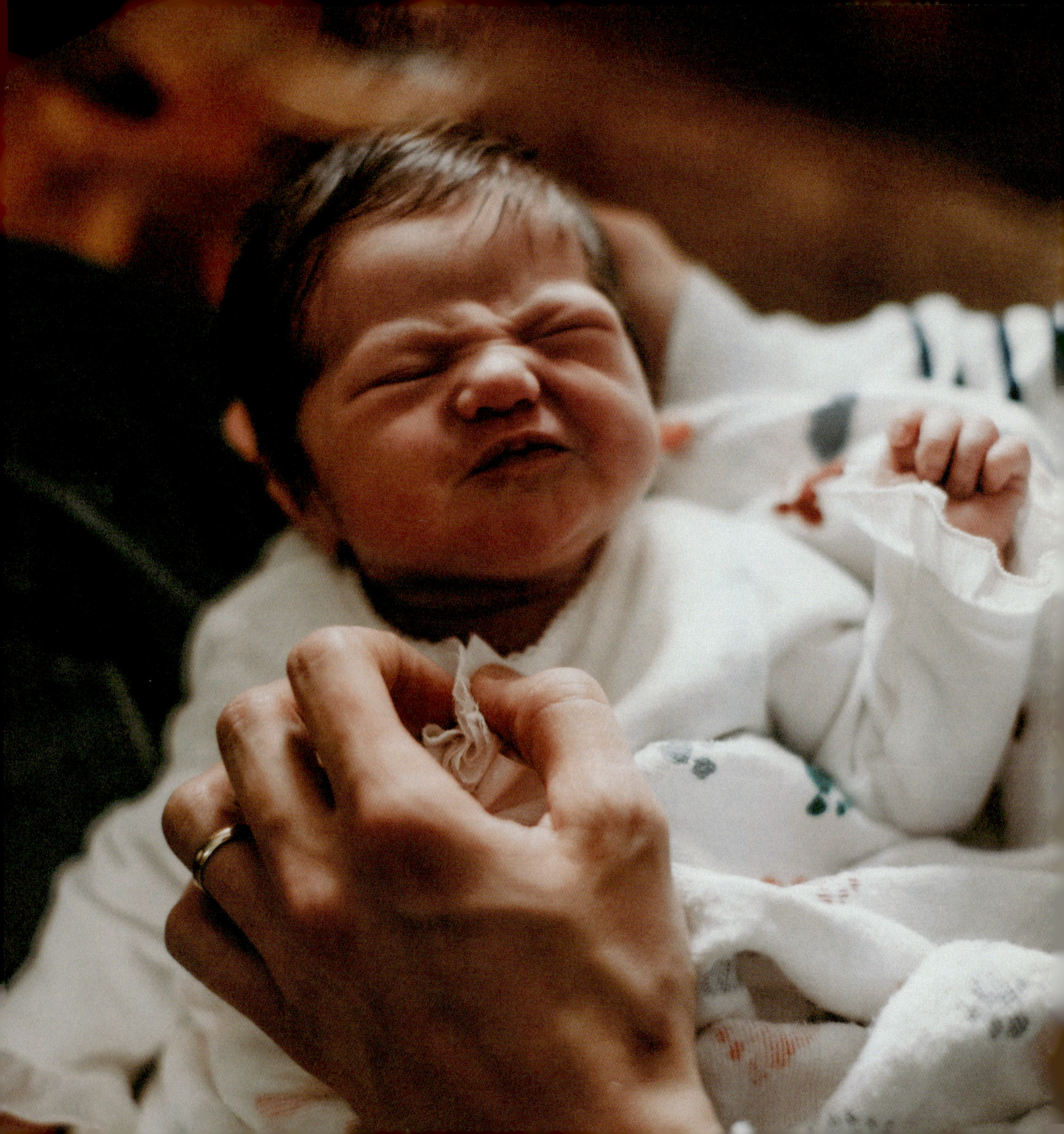

UNDERWEAR

It's all maternity bras and big pants.

There's nothing that destroys your femininity

like a pack of disposable knickers.

UNDERWEAR

An ever changing body means

plenty of retail therapy.

Beautiful shapewear is your friend.

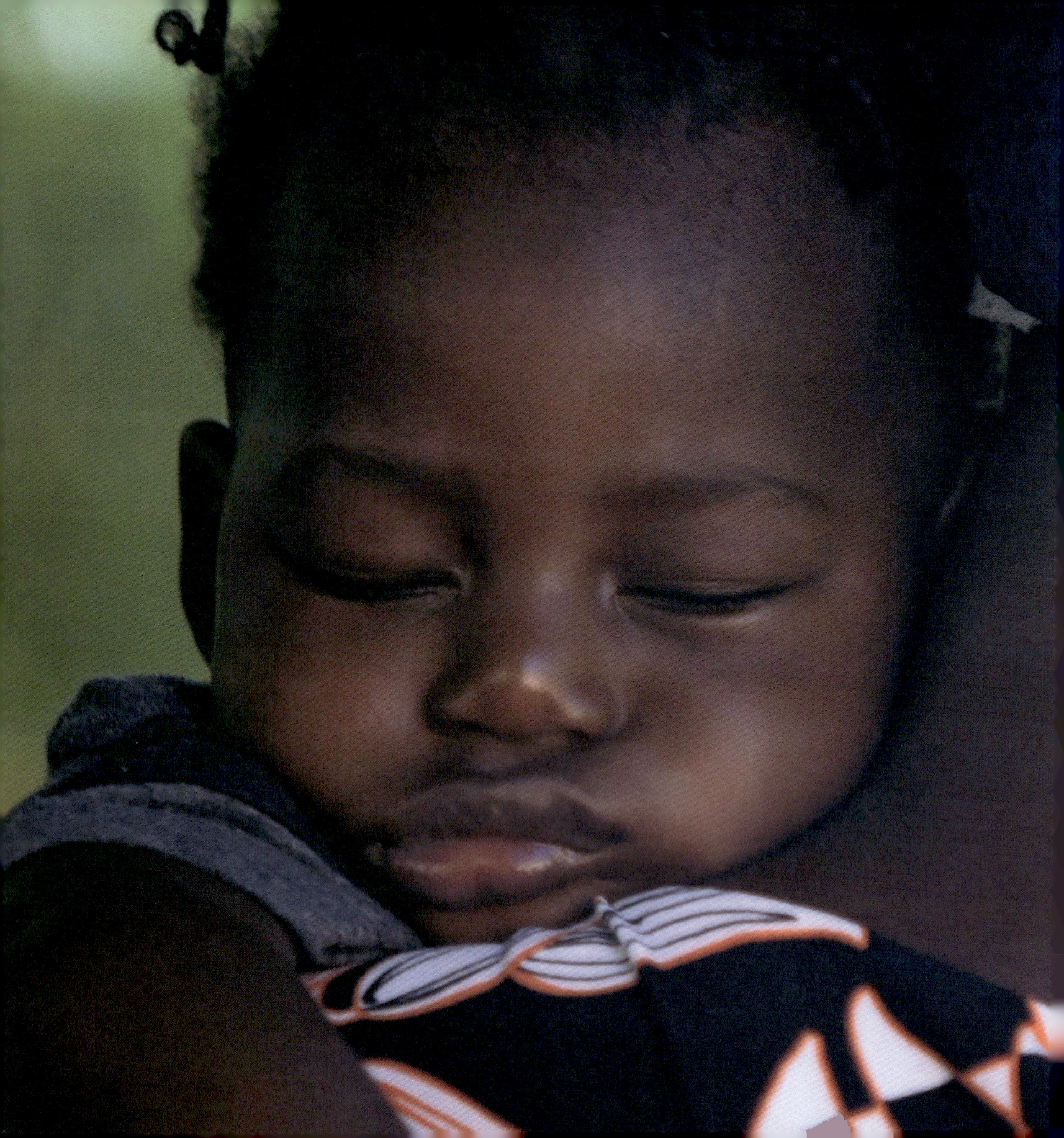

VEHICLE

Out with your sporty roadster and in with car seats and crumbs everywhere.

VEHICLE

How invincible you feel in your SUV with cavernous boot for buggy and a ton of other essential stuff you never knew you needed.

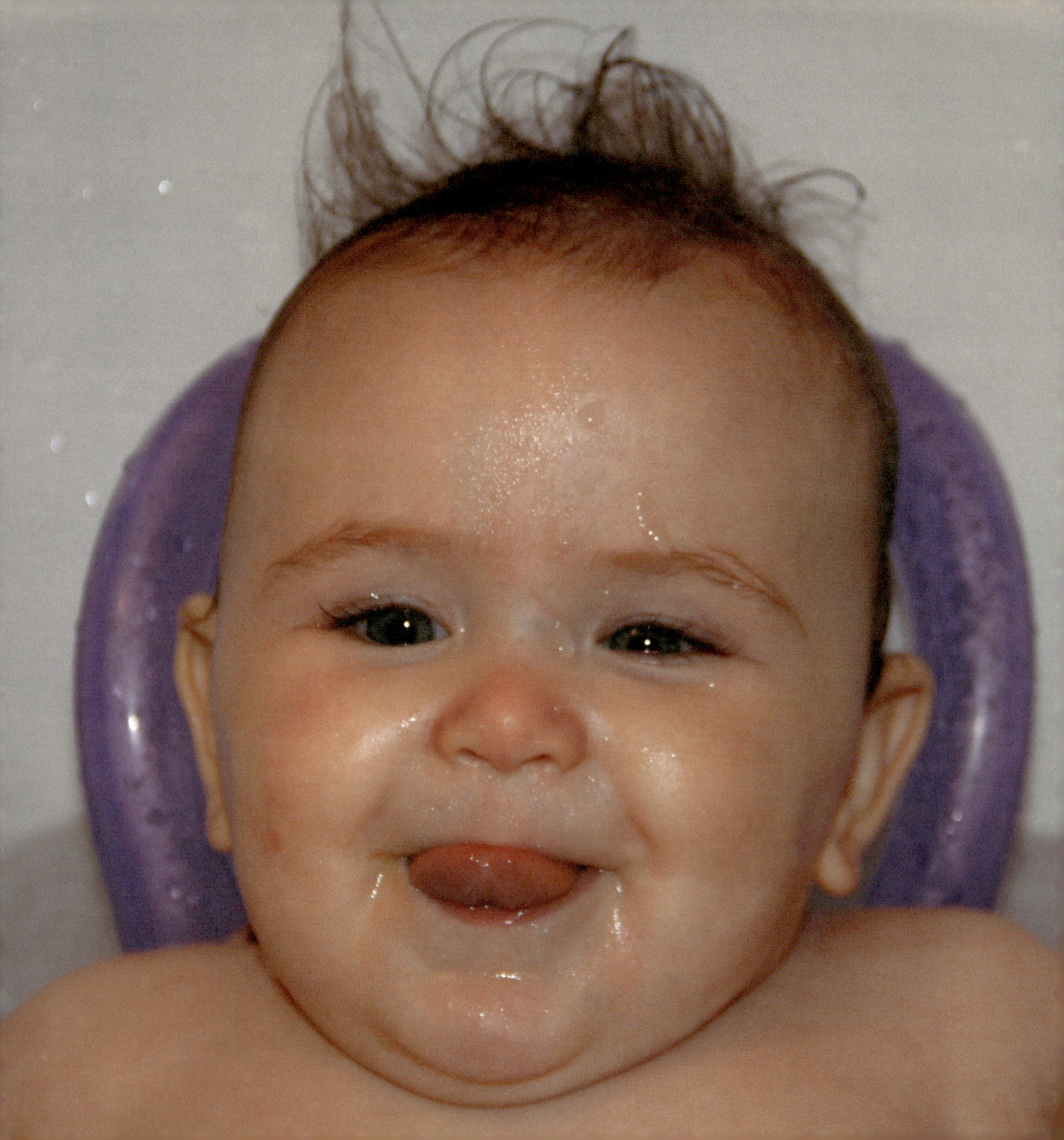

WET WIPES

Bulk buy now.

You're going to go through a ton of these

and be dependant long after junior needs them.

WET WIPES

How did you live without these before?

They're the ultimate all areas

multi tasking cleaning device!

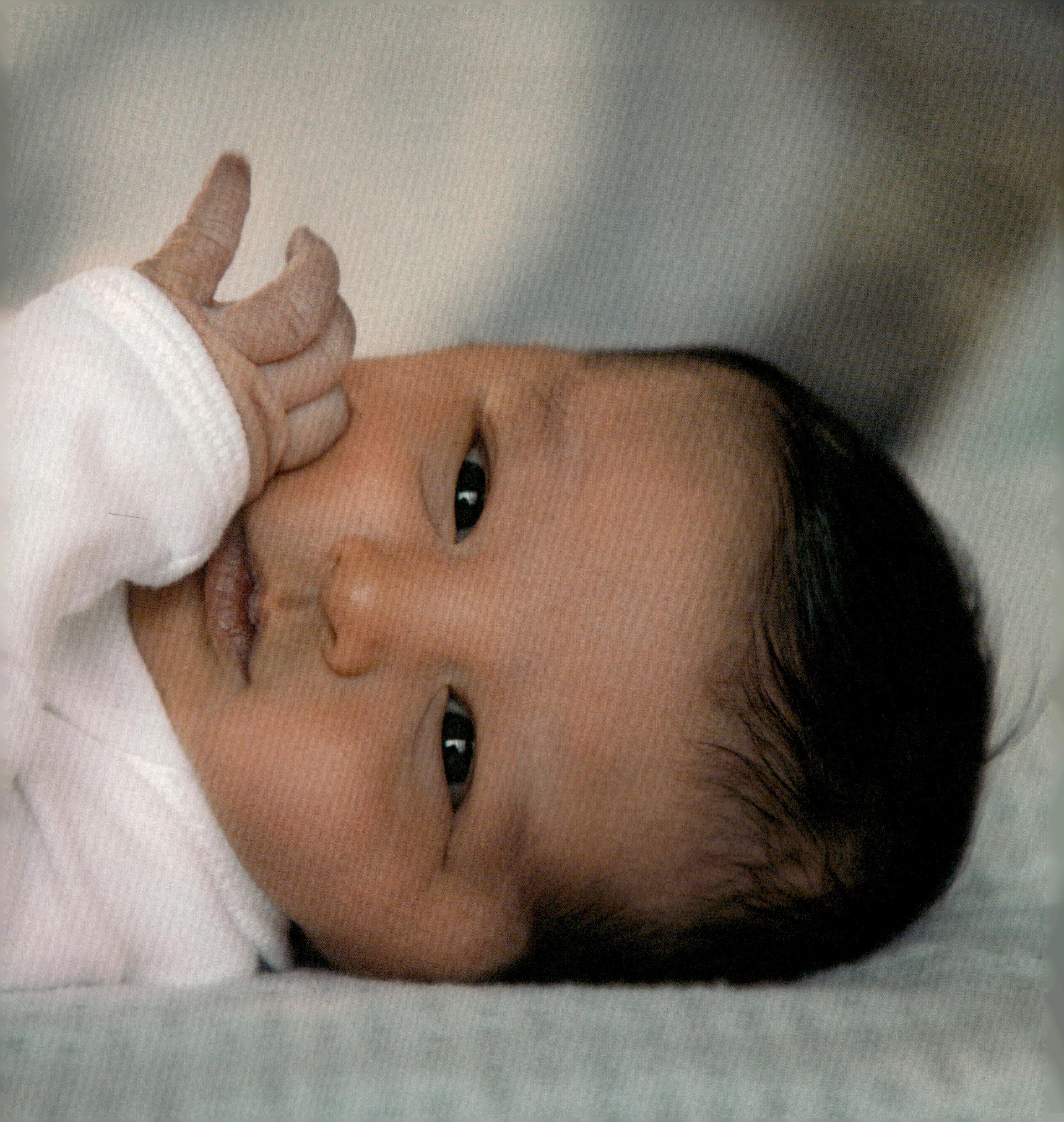

'X'

Represents the number 10

which is a size you'll never be again.

'X'

Also represents a kiss

which is what you'll find yourself

doing constantly to your baby.

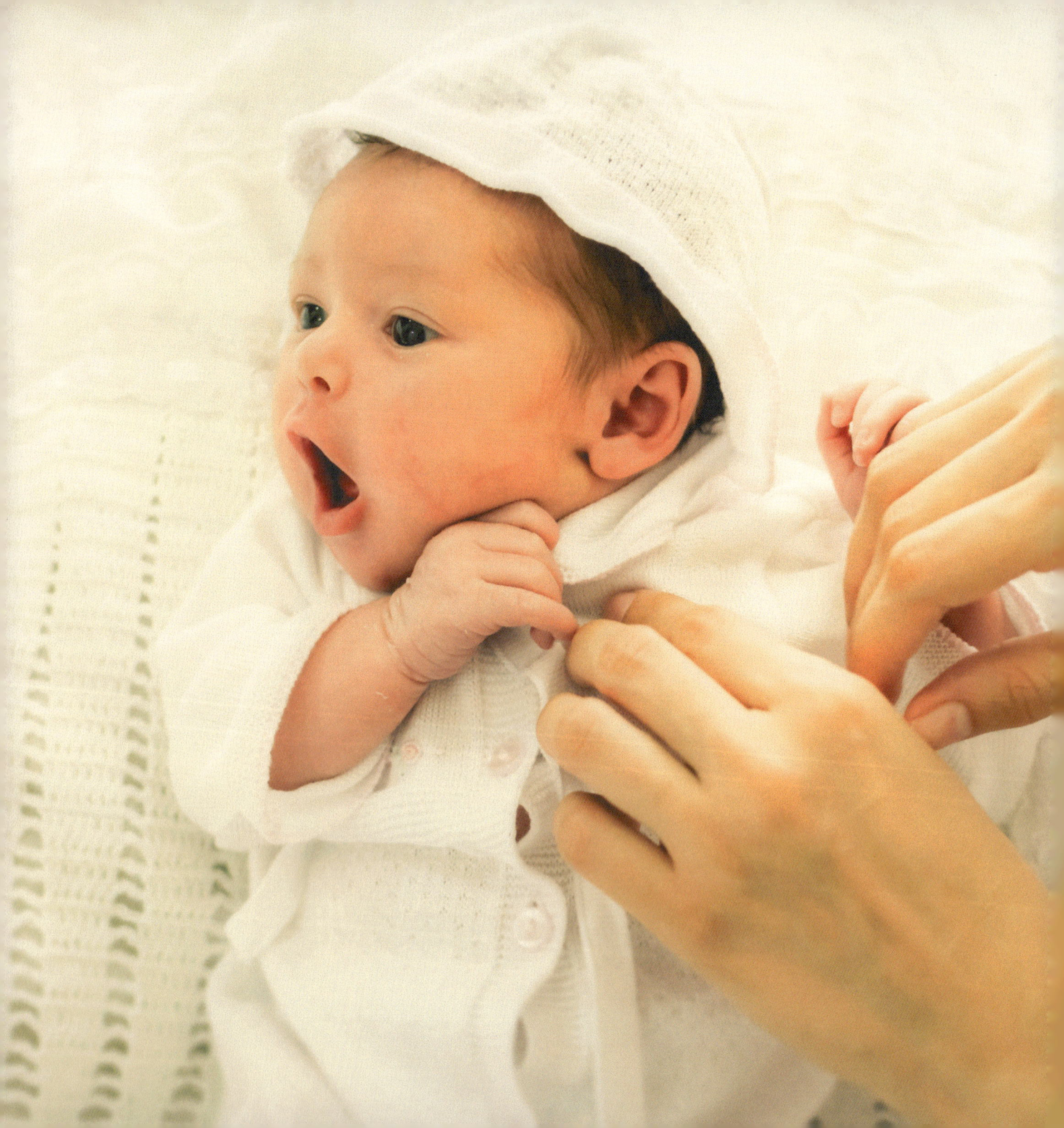

YOU

Your needs and desires hit the bottom of the pile after baby, partner, cleaning, shopping, laundry…

YOU

You have a whole new world to explore and will discover strengths, joys and love you never could imagine.

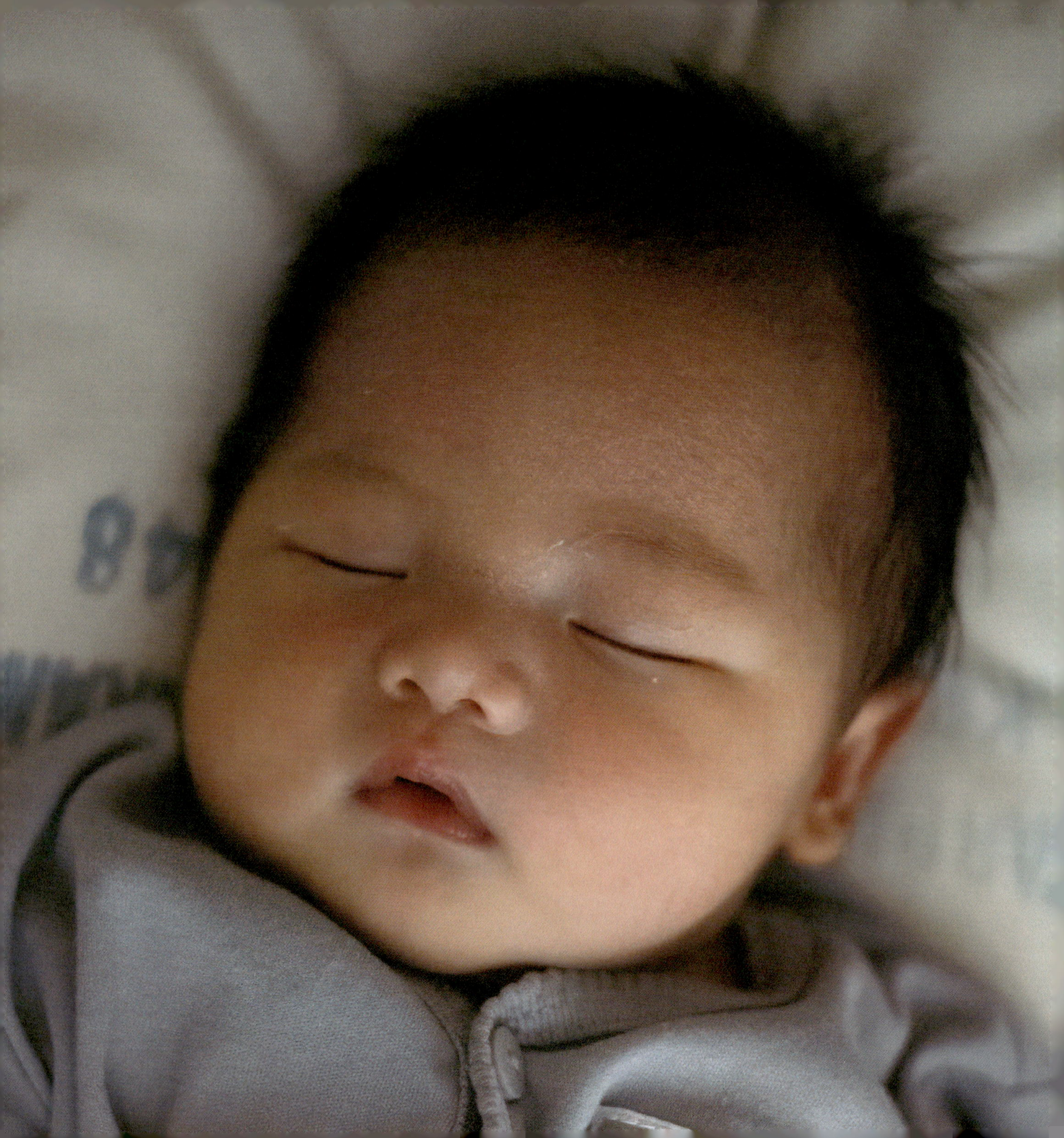

'Zzz'

A full uninterrupted 8 hours is a thing of the past.

You thought work was exhausting?

This is a whole new league!

'Zzz'

More desired, appreciated and cherished than it has ever been. You're amazed at how much you can achieve on so little sleep!

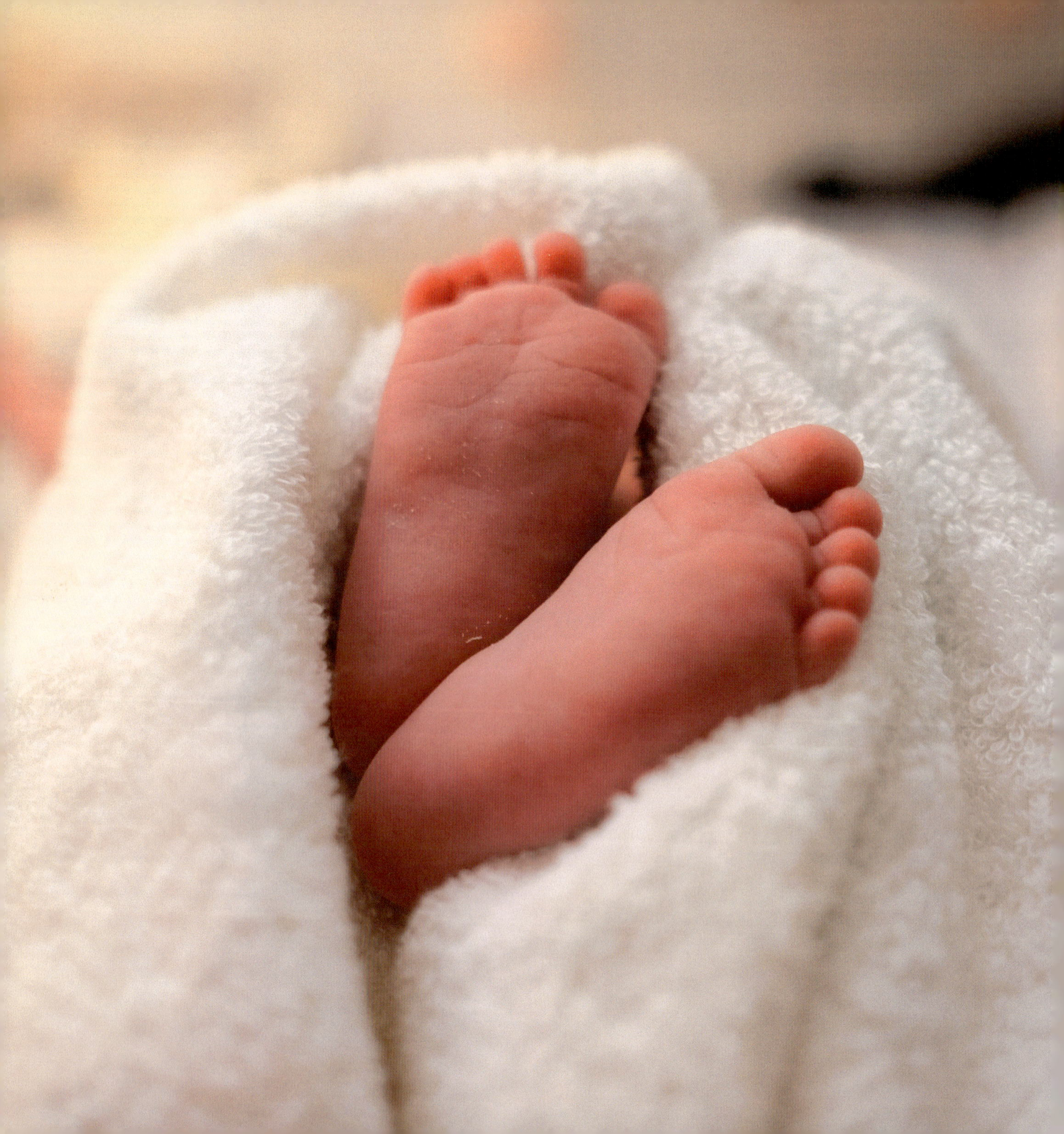

With thanks to the following photographers.

Cover photo: Minnie Zhou

Page 1: Jason Sung

Page 4: Garrett Jackson

Page 6: Kelly Sikkema

Page 8: Walaa Khaleel

Page 10: Minnie Zhou

Page 12: Katie Smith

Page 14: Paul Hanaoka

Page 16: Kazuend

Page 18: Zach Kadolph

Page 20: Minnie Zhou

Page 22: Minnie Zhou

Page 24: Katie Smith

Page 26: Hessam Nabavi

Page 28: Pranav Kumar Jain

Page 30: Minnie Zhou

Page 32: Jonathan Borba

Page 34: Katie Smith

Page 36: Nyana Stoica

Page 38: Minnie Zhou

Page 40: Mindy Olson P

Page 42: Sebastian Latorre

Page 44: Brytny.com

Page 46: Zach Vessels

Page 48: Shalev Cohen

Page 50: Gustavo Cultivo

Page 52: Felipe Salgado

Page 54: Reynardo Etenia Wongso

Page 56: Marcel Fagin

I hope you enjoyed my book and found it relatable!
If so, I'd love it if you could revisit your order or go to my Amazon.co.uk
Author page 'Sally Bignall Parenting Books' and leave a review, thanks.

Printed in Great Britain
by Amazon